# POEMS TO ENJOY: BOOK ONE

## Chosen and Edited by Verner Bickley

Proverse Hong Kong

Poems to Enjoy: Book 1 (Third Edition)

**VERNER BICKLEY, MBE, PhD,** is a well-known "voice", educationist, and adjudicator, who has held director-level positions in Universities and Government Departments. He is Chairman of the English-Speaking Union (HK) and Co-Founder of the International Proverse Prize for unpublished writing. He travels frequently to judge public-speaking competitions and regularly adjudicates verse and prose speaking and reading, as well as drama and choral speaking.

Dr Bickley's series of graded poetry anthologies – **POEMS TO ENJOY** – is a well-established tool for learning and teaching English at all levels. The five books are each accompanied by an audio recording of poems in the book. The recordings assist pronunciation and help those preparing for solo verse speaking and reading, duo and group-work and choral-speaking in Speech Festivals. They also enhance reading experience. Useful notes and a teaching guide are also included.

Taken as a whole, this five-book series is suitable for all students, teachers and parents. **Book 1** can be used and enjoyed by Primary 1-3 students and **Book 2** by Primary 4-6 students. **Book 3** can be used and enjoyed by Secondary 1-2 students, **Book 4** by Secondary 3-4 students and **Book 5** by secondary 5-6 students. Students, parents and teachers will enjoy and find useful Dr Bickley's selection of poems and the lively readings presented in the recording.

Parents will welcome this book, which gives them the opportunity to read aloud with their children.

THIS BOOK IS A PERENNIAL FAVOURITE.

# POEMS TO ENJOY

# BOOK ONE

## AN ANTHOLOGY OF POEMS

### FOR PRIMARY STUDENTS AND READERS

*WITH TEACHING AND LEARNING NOTES AND GUIDE*

**CHOSEN AND EDITED BY DR VERNER BICKLEY, MBE, PhD (Lond.), MA, BA (Hons), DipEd, LRAM, LGSM, FCIL, FRSA**

Proverse Hong Kong

Poems to Enjoy: Book 1 (Third Edition)

Poems to Enjoy, Book One
Chosen and Edited by Verner Bickley
With teaching notes by Verner Bickley
4th edition, published in Hong Kong by Proverse Hong Kong, November 2016.
Copyright © Verner Bickley, November 2016.
ISBN: 978-988-8228-63-8
Available from: https://www.createspace.com/6412741

Enquiries: Proverse Hong Kong, P. O. Box 259, Tung Chung Post Office, Tung Chung, Lantau Island, New Territories, Hong Kong SAR, China.
Email: proverse@netvigator.com   Website: www.proversepublishing.com

Illustrations & cover design copyright © Proverse Hong Kong.
Page design by Proverse Hong Kong. Cover design, Proverse Hong Kong and Artist Hong Kong Company.

The right of Verner Bickley to be identified as the anthologiser and editor of this work has been asserted by him in accordance with the Copyright, Designs and Patents Act 1988.

All rights reserved. No part of this publication may be reproduced, stored in a retrieval system, or transmitted, in any form or by any means, electronic, mechanical, photocopying, recording or otherwise, without the prior written permission of the publisher or publisher and author. The book is sold subject to the condition that it shall not, by way of trade or otherwise, be lent, re-sold, hired out or otherwise circulated without the publisher's prior written consent in any form of binding or cover other than that in which it is published and without a similar condition including this condition being imposed on the subsequent owner or purchaser. Please contact Proverse Hong Kong in writing, to request any and all permissions (including but not restricted to republishing, inclusion in anthologies, translation, reading, performance and use as set pieces in examinations and festivals).

*Poems to Enjoy*, Book One was first published in the United Kingdom in 1960,
by University of London Press Ltd, copyright © Verner Bickley 1960,
with Teaching Notes in a separate volume. Copyright © Verner Bickley 1960.
Some of the poems in the first, third and this fourth edition of *Poems to Enjoy* appeared in *Poems To Enjoy*, Book 1, second edition, part of a three book series. The 3rd edition was accompanied by two audio CDs of recordings of all the poems in the book.

---

Proverse Hong Kong

British Library Cataloguing in Publication Data (for 3rd pbk edition)

Poems to enjoy.
Book 1. -- 3rd ed.
1. English poetry. 2. Oral interpretation of poetry--
Juvenile literature. 3. English poetry--Study and teaching
(Elementary) 4. English language--Study and teaching--
Foreign speakers.
I. Bickley, Verner Courtenay.
821'.008-dc23

ISBN-13: 9789888167548

# Acknowledgements

For permission to use copyright material thanks are due to: The Clarendon Press for 'Trumpet and Drum,' 'Knock at the Door', 'A Little Talk,' 'The Goldfish' and 'As I Looked Out', all by Herbert Strang and taken from *50 Poems for Infants*, and for 'Heigh-Ho' by M. Ashworth from *Treasures of English Verse*; Messrs William Collins, Sons & Co. Ltd. For 'Timothy Too' by Dorothy King and 'If I Met' by Queenie Scott Hopper, both taken from *Stardust and Silver*; Messrs Evans Brothers Limited for 'Hide and Seek' by Phyllis Drayson, 'My Toys', 'Pussy Cat and Puppy Dog' and 'Getting Up' by Lilian McCrea, 'To Let' by D. Newey Johnson and 'The Balloon Man' by E. Herbert, all from *Come, Follow Me*; Mrs Joan Bennett for 'Sheep and Lambs', 'Drowsy Flies', 'Rubadubdub' and 'Dickyducks' all by Rodney Bennett and taken from *The Playway of Speech Training* published by Messrs Evans Brothers Limited; Miss Mona Swann for her poems 'Ding-Dong! Ting a Ling!' and 'Clapping Rhyme', both from *Trippingly on the Tongue* published by Messrs Macmillan & Co Ltd; Messrs. J. B. Cramer & Co. Ltd. London for 'The Three Little Pigs' by Sir Alfred Scott-Gatty; Messrs A & C. Black Ltd. for 'The Crow,' 'At Play', 'The Drum' and 'Dance in a Ring' by W. Kingdon-Ward from *Rhymes and Jingles*, 'The Postman', 'Walking With A Swing' and 'Galloping' by Clive Sansom, 'Running', 'Skipping' and 'Stirring' by Ruth Large, all from *Speech Rhymes* and 'Hamering' by Clive Sansom from *Acting Rhymes;* McDougall's Educational Co, Ltd.. for 'The Camel' and 'Stepping Stones' by Irene Thompson from *Speech Training Verses and Melodies* by Irene Thompson and Marjorie Davies; Mr Robert Graves for his poem 'A Cough'; The Society of Authors as the Literary Representative of the Estate of the late Miss Rose Fyleman for 'Mrs Minnitt' and 'The Goblin'; Messrs Ginn and Company Ltd; for 'Bounce the Ball' by Freda Parsons from *Gateway of Speech*; Messrs Cambridge University Press for 'O, look at the Moon!' by Eliza Lee Follen from *Book of Poetry for Children*, compiled by Kenneth Graham; Mr. Wilfred Thorley for his poem 'Song for a Ball-Game', and Mrs B. Lumsden Milne and Messrs Macmillan and Co., Ltd, for 'Tigers' from *Modern Speech Rhythm Exercises* Book 1.

It certain cases it has not been possible to trace the copyright holders, but full acknowledgement of any rights not mentioned here will be made in subsequent editions if notification is received.

## To the Student

The poems in this little book have been chosen for you to enjoy. Sometimes your teacher or one of your parents will read them to you while you listen. Sometimes, with your teacher's help, or with one of your parents, you might want to say some of the lines yourself.

Later, when you know the poems well, you will be able to act the stories told in some of them. You will be able to dance and skip to the lines as your teacher, or a group of classmates speaks them.

Most of the poems are very easy to understand, but there are a few more difficult ones which you teacher will explain to you. Don't worry if you find you do not fully understand a poem right away. As you hear more and more poems spoken and as you begin to read more yourself, the difficulties will gradually disappear.

I hope that you will sometimes bring to class poems that you have found yourself. Perhaps, after a time, your group might like to make a collection of poems to put in the Library or English Corner.

I hope you have fun with this book. If you do, it will have been well worth making it for you.

# Contents

| | | |
|---|---|---|
| Acknowledgements | | 5 |
| To the Student | | 6 |

### PART ONE: POEMS TO SPEAK

| TITLE | AUTHOR | PAGE |
|---|---|---|
| Trumpet and Drum | Herbert Strang | 12 |
| Fishes | Anonymous | 12 |
| Ding, Dong, Bell | Anonymous | 13 |
| Hop, Hop, Hop | Anonymous | 13 |
| Knock at the Door | Herbert Strang | 14 |
| The Moon | Eliza Lee Follen | 14 |
| When are you going, My Little Cat? | Traditional | 15 |
| The Rain | Anonymous | 15 |
| Timothy Too | Dorothy King | 16 |
| Oh where and Oh where? | Anonymous | 16 |
| A Rhyme for Washing Hands | Traditional | 17 |
| Hey, Diddle, Diddle! | Traditional | 17 |
| My Toys | Lilian McCrea | 18 |
| A Riddle | Traditional | 19 |
| Hide and Seek | Phyllis Drayson | 19 |
| Three Little Kittens | Traditional | 20 |
| To Let | D. Newey-Johnson | 21 |
| How Many Days has My Baby to Play? | Traditional | 21 |
| Pussy-Cat and Puppy-Dog | Lilian McCrea | 22 |
| Ding-Dong! Ting-a-Ling! | Mona Swann | 22 |
| Sheep and Lambs | Rodney Bennett | 23 |
| Drowsy Flies | Rodney Bennett | 23 |
| A Little Talk | Herbert Strang | 24 |
| If I Met | Queenie Scott-Hopper | 24 |
| "Bow Wow", Says the Dog | Traditional | 25 |
| Tippy Tiptoe | Anonymous | 25 |
| The Three Little Pigs | Sir Alfred Scott- | 26 |

| | | |
|---|---|---|
| Just Like Me | Gatty Traditional | 28 |
| Blow the Fire | Traditional | 28 |
| The Crow | Winifred Kingdon-Ward | 29 |
| Bells go Ding Dong! | Traditional | 30 |
| Hammer, Hammer, Hammer | Traditional | 30 |
| The Ferryman | Christina Rossetti | 31 |
| The Song of the Engine | H. Worseley-Benison | 31 |
| Windy Nights | Robert Louis Stevenson | 33 |
| The Squirrel | Anonymous | 34 |
| Wee Willie Winkie | Traditional | 35 |
| There was an Old Woman | Traditional | 36 |
| Ring the Gong | Traditional | 36 |
| The Old Woman in the Basket | Traditional | 37 |
| Bat, Bat | Traditional | 37 |
| Flippetty, Clippetty | Traditional | 38 |
| A Hippity Hippity Hop! | Traditional | 38 |
| What do I See? | Traditional | 39 |
| Hickety Pickety? | Traditional | 39 |
| Round the Roundabout | Traditional | 40 |
| Tigers | B. Lumsden-Milne | 40 |
| Another Riddle | Traditional | 42 |
| The Goldfish | Herbert Strang | 42 |
| As I Looked Out | Herbert Strang | 43 |
| Three Little Mice | Traditional | 44 |
| Ducks | Mary Daunt | 45 |
| Whistle | Anonymous | 46 |
| What Does the Bee Do? | Christina Rossetti | 46 |
| The Spider's Web | Charlotte Druitt Cole | 47 |
| Clocks and Watches | Traditional | 48 |
| Flying Kites | E. B. M. Watson | 49 |
| Who Has Seen the Wind? | Christina Rossetti | 50 |

## PART TWO: POEMS TO ACT AND DANCE

| TITLE | AUTHOR | PAGE |
|---|---|---|
| The Elves' Dance | John Bennett | 52 |
| Incey Wincey Spider | Anonymous | 52 |
| The Swing | Robert Louis Stevenson | 53 |
| The Postman | Clive Sansom | 53 |
| The Little Mice | Anonymous | 54 |
| Stepping Stones | Irene Thompson | 54 |
| Dickyducks | Rodney Bennett | 56 |
| The Pancake | Christina Rossetti | 56 |
| Getting Up | Lilian McCrea | 57 |
| The Balloon Man | E. Herbert | 58 |
| The Little Piggies | Thomas Hood | 60 |
| Rubadubdub! | Rodney Bennett | 62 |
| Here We Go Dancing | Traditional | 63 |
| Paddling | Traditional | 64 |
| The Camel | Irene Thompson | 64 |
| A Cough | Robert Graves | 65 |
| One, Two, Buckle My Shoe! | Traditional | 66 |
| Hopping Frog | Christina Rossetti | 66 |
| The Little Piggy-Wig | D'Arcy Wentworth Thompson | 67 |
| Finger Play | Anonymous | 68 |
| Mr Minnitt | Rose Fyleman | 69 |
| The Goblin | Rose Fyleman | 70 |
| Hark! Hark! The Dogs Do Bark! | Traditional | 71 |
| Is John Smith Within? | Traditional | 71 |
| Finger Game 1 | Traditional | 72 |
| Finger Game 2 | Traditional | 72 |
| A Face Game | Traditional | 74 |
| Here We Go! (A Dance) | Traditional | 74 |
| When I was a Lady! | Traditional | 74 |
| At Play | Winifred Kingdon-Ward | 75 |
| Dance in a Ring | Winifred Kingdon-Ward | 76 |

## POEMS TO ACT AND DANCE

| TITLE | AUTHOR | PAGE |
|---|---|---|
| The Drum | Winifred Kingdon-Ward | 77 |
| Heigh Ho! | M. Ashworth | 78 |
| Song for a Ball-Game | Winifred Thorley | 79 |
| Clapping Rhyme | Mona Swann | 81 |
| Looby Loo | Traditional | 81 |
| When the Wind is in the East | Traditional | 82 |
| Skipping | Ruth Large | 82 |
| Walking with a Swing | Clive Sansom | 83 |
| Running | Ruth Large | 83 |
| Stirring | Ruth Large | 84 |
| Galloping | Clive Sansom | 84 |
| Marching | Traditional | 84 |
| Ting-a-Ling-Bone! | Traditional | 85 |
| Why is Pussy in Bed? | Traditional | 85 |
| Kings Came Riding | Charles Williams | 87 |
| Bounce the Ball | Freda Parsons | 89 |
| Clapping Game | Traditional | 90 |
| Sing me a Song | Christina Rossetti | 90 |
| The Animals and the Ark | Traditional | 91 |
| Hammering | Clive Sansom | 92 |
| Who's that Ringing? | Traditional | 93 |

| | |
|---|---|
| Teaching and Learning Notes and Guide | 95 |
| Notes on the audio recording: Track contents, playing times, Readers, and ISRC Numbers. | 119 |
| About Proverse Hong Kong | 122 |
| About the Editor-Anthologiser | 123 |
| About The Proverse Prize | 125 |
| Selected books published by / available through Proverse Hong Kong | 127 |

# PART ONE

# POEMS TO SPEAK

## TRUMPET AND DRUM

Michael has a drum, and he knows how to play,
A red drum, a fine drum, very bright and gay.

"Rub-a-dub-dub!" says Michael's drum.
"Boom! Zoom! Zoom! Here we come!
Rub-a-dub-dub! – Who cares?
All the way up the stairs.

*Herbert Strang*

## FISHES

One, two, three, four, five,
Catching fishes all alive.
Why did you let them go?
Because they bit my finger so.

*Anonymous*

## DING DONG BELL

Ding, dong, bell,
Pussy's in the well!
Who put her in?
Little Tommy Thin.

*Anonymous*

## HOP, HOP, HOP

Once I saw a little bird
Come hop, hop, hop;
So I cried, "Little bird,
Will you stop, stop, stop?"
I was going to the window
To say, "How do you do?"
But he shook his little tail
and away he flew.

*Anonymous*

## KNOCK AT THE DOOR

Mr Wind he knocks at the door;
Mr Wind he rattles the blind;
Mr Wind he creeps up the stair.
When I go to bed, he's not far behind,
And he whistles and blows all round my head,
And I hear him knocking when I'm in bed.
"Come in, Mr Wind," but he
Never comes in.
"What's that, Mr Wind?" but
He never replies.
He dances alone, all by himself,
Under the wild, dark skies

*Herbert Strang*


## THE MOON

O, look at the moon!
She is shining up there.
O mother, she looks
Like a lamp in the air!

*Eliza Lee Follen*

# WHERE ARE YOU GOING, MY LITTLE CAT?

Where are you going,
My little cat?

I am going to town,
To get me a hat.

What! A hat for a cat!
A cat get a hat!
Who ever saw a cat with a hat?

*Traditional*

# THE RAIN

Rain on the green grass,
And rain on the tree,
And rain on the house-top,
But not upon me!

*Anonymous*

## TIMOTHY TOO

Timothy Too once dropped his shoe
In a great big tub that was full of glue;
So he jumped in, saying, "I'll soon get you!"
But the shoe stuck fast – and Timothy too!

*Dorothy King*


## OH WHERE AND OH WHERE?

Oh where and oh where is my little dog gone?
Oh where and oh where can he be?
With his tail cut short and his ears cut long.
Oh where and oh where can he be?

*Anonymous*

## A RHYME FOR WASHING HANDS

Wash, hands, wash,
Daddy's gone to plough.
Splash, hands, splash,
They're all washed now.

*Traditional*

## HEY, DIDDLE, DIDDLE!

Hey, diddle, diddle!
The cat and the fiddle,
The cow jumped over the moon;
The little dog laughed
To see such sport,
And the dish ran away with the spoon.

*Traditional*

## MY TOYS

My red engine goes chuff-chuff-choo!
    chuff-chuff-choo!
My shiny drum goes rum-tum-tum!
    rum-tum-tum!
My teddy bear goes grr…grr…grr…!
And my wooden bricks go clitter-clatter,
    clitter-clatter,
        rattle-bang-BUMP!

*Lilian McCrea*

## A RIDDLE

I have a little sister, they call her Peep,
She wades the water so deep, deep, deep;
She climbs the mountains, high, high, high;
Poor little creature, she has but one eye.

*Traditional*



## HIDE AND SEEK

Baby loves to play with me,
Peek-a-boo! Peek-a-boo!
She goes and hides behind a tree,
I see you! I see you!

Baby is so very wee,
Hiding's easy as can be!

*Phyllis Drayson*

## THREE LITTLE KITTENS

Three little kittens
Lost their mittens
And they began to cry,
"Oh, Mother, dear,
We sadly fear
Our mittens we have lost!"
"What! Lost your mittens,
You naughty kittens?
Then you shall have no pie!
"Meow! Meow! Meow!"

Three little kittens,
They found their mittens,
And they began to cry,
"Oh, Mother, dear,
See here, see here,
Our mittens we have found!"
"What! Found your mittens,
You darling kittens?
Then you shall have some pie!"
"Purr, purr, purr."

*Traditional*

## TO LET

Two little beaks went tap! tap! tap!
Two little shells went crack! crack! crack!
Two fluffy chicks peeped out, and oh,
They liked the look of the big world so,
That they left their houses without a fret
And two little shells are now TO LET.

*D. Newey-Johnson*

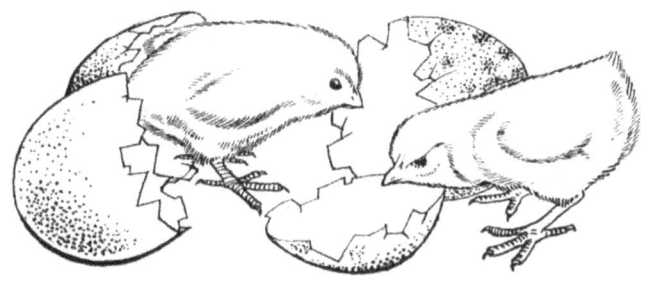

## HOW MANY DAYS HAS MY BABY TO PLAY?

How many days has my baby to play?
Saturday, Sunday, Monday,
Tuesday, Wednesday, Thursday, Friday,
Saturday, Sunday, Monday.

*Traditional*

## PUSSY-CAT AND PUPPY-DOG

Mee-ow, mee-ow,
Here's a little pussy-cat,
With furry, furry, fur,
Stroke her very gently
And she'll purr, purr, purr.

Bow-wow, bow-bow,
Here's a little puppy-dog
With a wiggly-waggly tail,
Pat him and he'll wag it
With a wiggy-wag-wag
And a waggy-wag-wag.

*Lilian McCrea*


## DING-DONG! TING-A-LING!
"Ding-dong! Ting-a-ling!"
"What do you bring?"
"Songs for singing, bells for ringing,
These things I bring."

*Mona Swann*

## SHEEP AND LAMBS

"Maa!" say the Lambs.
"Baa!" say their Mothers.
"So that's where you are!
Have you been far?"
"Ah!" say the Lambs.
"Baa!" say their Mothers.

*Rodney Bennett*


## DROWSY FLIES

ZzzzzZzzzzZzzzzZzzzz!
Drowsy flies are buzz-a-buzzing
On the sunlit glass:
"ZzzzzZzzzzZzzzzZzzzz!
Open all the windows, if you please,
And let us pass."

*Rodney Bennett*

## A LITTLE TALK

The big brown hen and Mrs Duck
Went walking out together;
They talked about all sorts of things—
The farmyard and the weather.
But all I heard was: "Cluck!
    Cluck! Cluck!"
And "Quack! Quack! Quack!"
    from Mrs Duck.

*Herbert Strang*


## IF I MET

If I met a crow,
I should say, "Caa-Caa!"
If I met a lamb,
I should say, "Baa-Baa!"
If I met a cow,
I should say, "Moo-Moo!"

*Queenie Scott-Hopper*

## "BOW-WOW SAYS THE DOG

"Bow-wow," says the dog,
"Mew-mew," says the cat;
"Grunt-grunt," goes the hog;
And "Squeak" goes the rat.

"Tu-whu," says the owl;
"Caw-caw," says the crow;
"Quack-quack," says the duck;
And "Moo," says the cow.

*Traditional*


## TIPPY TIPTOE

Tippy, Tippy, Tiptoe
Here we go.
Tippy, Tippy, Tiptoe
To and fro.
Tippy, Tippy, Tiptoe
Through the house
Tippy, Tippy, Tiptoe
Like a little mouse.

*Anonymous*

## THE THREE LITTLE PIGS

A jolly old pig once lived in a sty,
    And three little piggies had she;
And she waddled about, saying,
    "Umph! Umph! Umph!
While the little ones said, "Wee! Wee!"

"My dear little brothers," said one of the brats,
    "My dear little piggies," said he,
"Let us all for the future say,
    'Umph! Umph! Umph!"
"Tis so childish to say, "Wee! Wee'!"

Then these three little piggies grew skinny and lean,
    And lean they might very well be;
For somehow they *couldn't* say,
    "Umph! Umph! Umph!
And they *wouldn't* say, "Wee! Wee! Wee!"

So after a time these little pigs died,
    They all died, 'tis easy to see,
From trying too hard to say,
    "Umph!" Umph! Umph!"
When they could only say, "Wee! Wee!"

Moral:
A moral there is to this little song,
    A moral that's easy to see;
Don't try while yet young to say,
    "Umph! Umph! Umph!"
For you only can say, "Wee! Wee!"

*Sir Alfred Scott-Gatty*

## JUST LIKE ME

I went up one pair of stairs,
    Just like me.
I went up two pairs of stairs,
    Just like me.
I went into a room.
    Just like me.
I looked out of a window.
    Just like me,
And there I saw a monkey.
    Just like me.

*Traditional*


## BLOW THE FIRE

*Blow* the fire,
*Blow* the fire,
Puff-puff-puff!

First you blow it *gently*,
And then you blow it *rough*.
Wh————! Wh———!

*Traditional*

## THE CROW

There was an old crow
Who lived in a tree—
Caw-caw-caw;
A funnier bird
I never did see—
Caw-caw-caw;
And that was all
He ever could say—
Caw-caw-caw
He always said it
Every day—
    Caw-caw-caw—
        Caw—
            Caw—
                C-a-w!

*Winifred Kingdon-Ward*

## BELLS GO DING DONG!

Bells go Ding, Dong!
Trains go Ting Tang!
Balls go Ping Pong!
Hammers go Cling Clang!

*Traditional*


## HAMMER, HAMMER, HAMMER

Hammer, hammer, hammer,
Hammer, hammer, hammer,
Hammer, hammer, hammer
On the hard, high road.

Sparks we're sending,
Roads we're mending,

Hammer, hammer, hammer,
Hammer, hammer, hammer,
Hammer, hammer, hammer
On the hard, high road.

*Traditional*

## THE FERRYMAN

Maid:  Ferry me across the water,
         Do boatman, do.
Man:   If you've a penny in your purse,
         I'll ferry you.
Maid:  I have a penny in my purse.
         And my eyes are blue;
         So ferry me across the water,
         Do, boatman, do.
Man:   Step into my ferry-boat,
         Be they black or blue,
         And for the penny in your purse
         I'll ferry you.

*Christina Rossetti*


## THE SONG OF THE ENGINE

With snort and pant the engine dragged
    Its heavy train uphill,
And puffed these words the while she puffed
    And laboured with a will:

"I think—I can—I think—I can,
I've got to reach the top.
I'm sure—I can—I will—get there
I sim-ply must-not stop."
At last the top was reached and passed,
    And then—how changed the song!

The wheels all joined in the engine's joy,
    As quickly she tore along!

"I knew I could do it, I knew I could win,
    Oh, rickety, rackety, rack!
And now for a roaring rushing race
    On my smooth and shining track!"

*H. Worsley-Benison*

## WINDY NIGHTS

Whenever the moon and stars are set,
    Whenever the wind is high,
All night long in the dark and wet
    A man goes riding by.
Late in the night when the fires are out
Why does he gallop and gallop about?

Whenever the trees are crying aloud
    And ships are tossed at sea,
By, on the highway, low and loud,
    By at a gallop goes he.
By at the gallop he goes, and then
By he comes back at the gallop again.

*Robert Louis Stevenson*

## THE SQUIRREL

Whiskey, frisky,
Hippity hop,
Up he goes
To the tree top!

Whirly, twirly,
Round and round,
Down he scampers
To the ground.

Furly, curly
What a tail!
Tall as a feather
Broad as a sail!

Where's his supper?
In the shell,
Snappity, crackity,
Out it fell.

*Anonymous*

## WEE WILLIE WINKIE

Wee Willie Winkie
Runs through the town.
Upstairs and downstairs
In his nightgown.
Rapping at the window,
Crying through the lock,
"Are the children in their beds?
It's past eight o'clock."

*Traditional*

## THERE WAS AN OLD WOMAN

There was an old woman,
And nothing she had,
And so this old woman
Was said to be mad.
She'd nothing to eat,
She'd nothing to wear,
She'd nothing to lose,
She'd nothing to fear,
She'd nothing to ask,
She'd nothing to give,
And when she did die,
She'd nothing to leave.

*Traditional*


## RING THE GONG

Ring the gong—ding dong,
Sing a song—sing song.
    Singing a song,
    Ringing the gong,
Ding-ling-dong, ding dong.

*Traditional*

## THE OLD WOMAN IN THE BASKET

There was an old woman went up in a basket,
Seventy times as high as the moon;
What she did there, I could not but ask it,
For in her hand she carried a broom.
"Old woman, old woman, old woman," said I,
Whither, oh whither, oh whither so high?
"To sweep the cobwebs from the sky,
And I shall be back again by and by."

*Traditional*


## BAT, BAT

Bat, bat, come under my hat,
And I'll give you a slice of bacon;
And when I bake, I'll give you a cake,
If I am not mistaken.

*Traditional*

## PLIPPETTY, CLIPPETTY

The rain comes pittering pattering down,
    Plippetty, plippetty, plop.
The farmer drives his horse to town,
    Clippetty, clippetty clop.
The rain comes pattering,
Horse goes clattering,
    Clippetty, clippetty, clop.

*Traditional*


## A HIPPITY HIPPITY HOP!

A hippity, hippity hop! Heighho!
Away to the blacksmith's shop we go,
If you have a pony,
That's lost a shoe,
You can get her another
All shining and new.
A hippity, hippity hop!

*Traditional*

# WHAT DO I SEE?

What do I see?
A bumble-bee
Sit on a rose
And wink at me!

What do you mean
By hum, hum, hum?
If you mean me,
I dare not come!

*Traditional*


# HICKETY PICKETY

Hickety Pickety, my black hen,
She lays eggs for gentlemen,
Sometimes nine, and sometimes ten,
Hickety, Pickety, my black hen.

*Traditional*

## ROUND THE ROUNDABOUT

All round the round-about the cars go round,
I stand by the round-about to see them going round.
Buses, cars and lorries, travelling up and down,
Going round the round-about, in and out of town.

*Traditional*


## TIGERS

I'd like to play with tigers,
The tigers in the Zoo;
But people tell me that would be
A dreadful thing to do.

Those tigers they would eat me,
And chew me up to bits;
And Father would be furious,
And Mother would have fits!

But I know some tigers,
As tame as tame can be;
And when I go to sleep at night
They come and play with me.

They lift me on their backs and I
Can ride them, fast or slow;
The tigers that I dream about
Are very nice to know!

*B. Lumsden-Milne*

## ANOTHER RIDDLE

There was a little green house,
And in the little green house
There was a little brown house.
And in the little brown house
There was a little yellow house,
And in the little yellow house
There was a little white house,
And in the little white house
There was a little heart.

*Traditional*


## THE GOLDFISH

Goldfish swimming in the pool
Where it's always dark and cool,
Tell me, would you like to be
A real little girl like me?
Not dressed up in your golden coat,
And there for ever made to float,
But with two feet to run like me?
Goldfish with your smiling eyes,
Are you very cold and wise?
Don't you want to run and play?

Would you really rather stay
Always in your shady pool
Down below the water cool,
Every day and every day?

*Herbert Strang*


## AS I LOOKED OUT

As I looked out on Saturday last,
A fat little pig went hurrying past.
Over his shoulders he wore a shawl,
Although it didn't seem cold at all.
I waved at him, but he didn't see,
For he never so much as looked at me.
Once again, when the moon was high,
I saw the little pig hurrying by;
Back he came at a terrible pace,
The moonlight shone on his little pink face,
And he smiled with a smile that was quite content.
But never I knew where that little pig went.

*Herbert Strang*

## THREE LITTLE MICE

Three little mice sat down to spin,
Pussy passed by and she peeped in.
"What are you doing, my little men?"
"We're making coats for gentlemen."
"Shall I come in and bite off your threads?"
"No, not, Miss Pussy, you'll snip off our heads."
"Oh, no, I'll not, I'll help you to spin."
"That may be so, but you don't come in."

*Traditional*

## DUCKS

Mother likes her black hen
That lays an egg and clucks.
Father likes his new car.
    But I like ducks.

    I like their fronts.
    I like their backs.
    I like their waddle.
    I like their 'Quacks'.

Bobby likes his toy train
With its yellow trucks.
Betty likes her baby doll.

    But I like ducks.

*Mary Daunt*

## WHISTLE

I want to learn to whistle,
I've always wanted to;
I fix my mouth to do it, but
The whistle won't come through.

I think perhaps it's stuck, and so
I try it once again;
Can people swallow whistles?
Where is my whistle then?

*Anonymous*


## WHAT DOES THE BEE DO?

What does the bee do?
    Bring home honey.
What does father do?
    Bring home money.
And what does mother do?
    Lay out the money.
And what does baby do?
    Eat up the honey.

*Christina Rossetti*

# THE SPIDER'S WEB

Spider! Spider!
    What are you spinning?
A cloak for a fairy
    I'm just beginning.

What is it made of,
    Tell me true?
Threads of moonshine,
    And pearls of dew.

When will the fairy
    Be wearing it?
To-night, when the glow-worm
    Lamps are lit.

Can I see her
    If I come peeping?
All good children
    Should then be sleeping.

*Charlotte Druitt Cole*

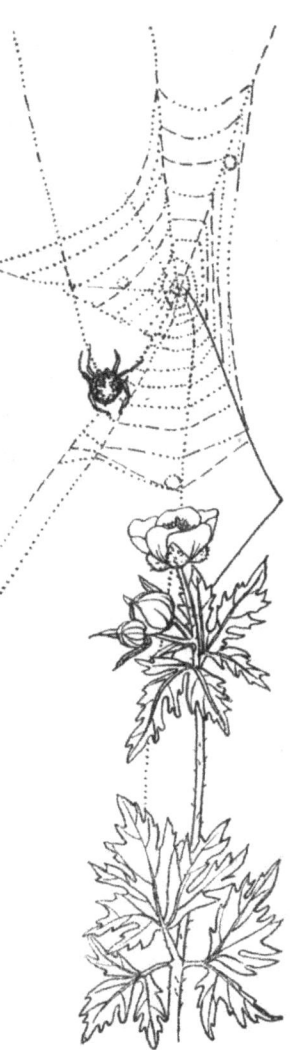

## CLOCKS AND WATCHES

Our great
Steeple clock
Goes TICK—TOCK.
TICK—TOCK;

Our small
Mantel clock
Goes Tick—Tack, Tick—Tack,
Tick—Tack, Tick—Tack;

Our little
Pocket watch
Goes tick-a-tacker, tick-a-tacker,
Tick-a-tacker, tick.

*Traditional*

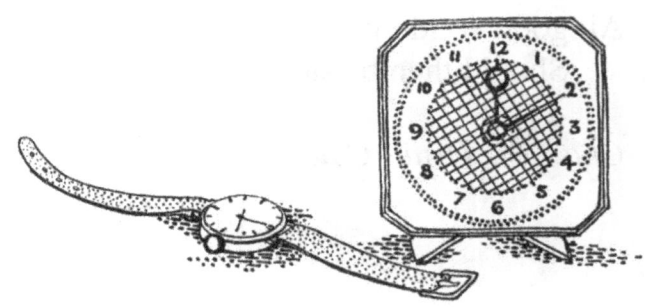

# FLYING KITES

*Girl*: Flying kites is fine;
See them soaring high.
Yours is higher than mine,
Right up in the sky.

*Boy*: Yours is by the pine,
Bright with the sunlight.
Now they fly in line.
What a pretty sight!

*Class*: Flying kites is fine;
See them soaring high.
Now they fly in line
Up into the sky.

*E.B.M. Watson*

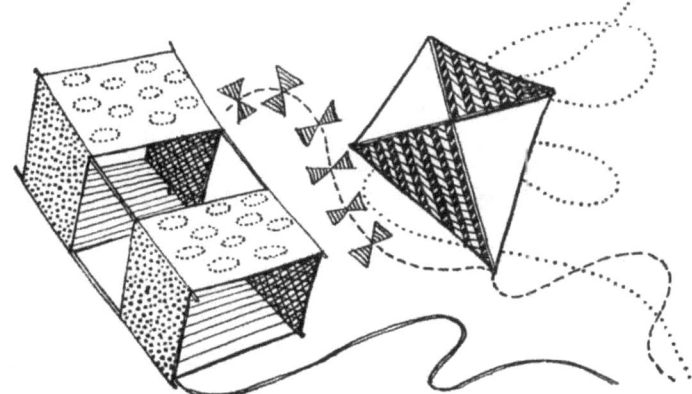

## WHO HAS SEEN THE WIND?

Who has seen the wind?
Neither I nor you:
But when the leaves hang trembling,
The wind is passing through.

Who has seen the wind?
Neither you nor I:
But when the trees bow down their heads,
The wind is passing by.

*Christina Rossetti*

# PART TWO

# POEMS TO ACT AND DANCE

## THE ELVES' DANCE

Round about, round about
In a fair ring-a,
Thus we dance, thus we dance,
And thus we sing-a.

Trip and go, to and fro
Over this green-a,
All about, in and out
Over this green-a.

*John Bennett*


## INCEY WINCEY SPIDER

Incey Wincey Spider climbed the water spout;
Down came the rain and washed poor spider out;
Out came the sunshine, dried up all the rain;
Incey Wincey Spider climbed up the spout again.

*Anonymous*

## THE SWING

How do you like to go up in a swing,
Up in the air so blue?
Oh, I do think it the pleasantest thing
Ever a child can do!

*Robert Louis Stevenson*


## THE POSTMAN

Rat-a-tat-tat, Rat-a-tat-tat,
    Rat-a-tat-tat-tatoo!
That's the way the Postman goes,
    Tat-a-tat-tat-tatoo!

Every morning at half past eight
    You hear a bang at the garden gate,
And Rat-a-tat-tat, Rat-a-tat-tat,
    Rat-at-tat-tat-tatoo!

*Clive Sansom*

## THE LITTLE MICE

The little mice are playing,
Playing, playing,
The little mice are playing
    Out in the barn.

The little mice are sleeping,
Sleeping, sleeping,
The little mice are sleeping
    Out in the barn.

*Anonymous*


## STEPPING STONES

Stepping stones!
    Stepping Stones!
        Splish!
            Splish!
                Splash!

Look and see,
    By the tree,
        Bright,
            Fish
                Flash!

Stepping stones!
    Stepping stones!
        Splish!
            Splish!
                Splash!

Shining Stones!
    Shaking stones!
        Splish!
            Splish!
                SPLASH!

*Irene Thompson*

## DICKY DUCKS

Quack! Quack! Quack!
From rick to stack
The ducks go marching now and then.
Double quick,
From stack to rick
They soon come quacking back again.
Quack! Quack! Quack!

*Rodney Bennett*


## THE PANCAKE

Mix a pancake,
Stir a pancake,
Pop it in the pan.

Fry the pancake,
Toss the pancake,
Catch it if you can.

*Christina Rossetti*

## GETTING UP

When I get up in the morning
I'll tell you what I do,
I wash my hands and I wash my face,
Splishity-splash, splishity-splash.
I clean my teeth till they're shining white,
Scrubbity-scrub, scrubbity-scrub,
Then I put on my clothes and brush my hair,
And runnity-run, I run downstairs.

*Lilian McCrea*

## THE BALLOON MAN

CHARACTERS:            PROPERTIES:
*Balloon Man*              *Coloured balloons*
*Mother*
*Three Children*

*Balloon Man:*
I stand here every afternoon,
Waiting for someone to buy a balloon.
Look at the colours bright and gay,
Just one penny is all you pay.
Plenty for all who come, have I,
Come and buy! Come and buy!

*First Child*:
I have a penny, Mother said,
So I think I'd like one of red.

*Second Child*:
I would like that one of green.
It is the prettiest that I've seen.

*Third Child*:
Lucky am I, please give me two,
One of yellow and one of blue.

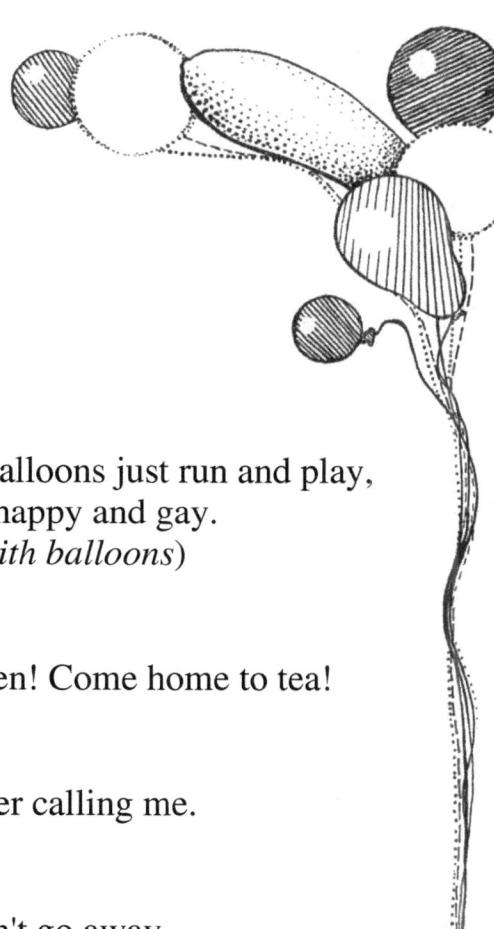

*Balloon Man*:
Now with your balloons just run and play,
I like to see you happy and gay.
(*Children play with balloons*)

*Mother*:
Children! Children! Come home to tea!

*First Child*:
That is my Mother calling me.

*All together*:
Balloon man, don't go away,
We'll come and see you another day.
*(Children run out saying" Good-bye"!)*

E. Herbert

## THE LITTLE PIGGIES

*Child*: Where are you going, you little pig?
*1st Pig:* I'm leaving my mother, I'm growing so big!
*Child*: So big, young pig!
So young, so big!
What, leaving your mother, you foolish young pig!

*Child:* Where are you going, you little pig?
*2nd Pig:* I've got a new spade and I'm going to dig.
*Child*: To dig, little pig!
A little pig dig!
Well, I never saw a pig with a spade that could dig!

*Child*: Where are you going, you little pig?
*3rd Pig*: Why, I'm going to have a nice ride in a gig!
*Child*: In a gig, little pig!
What, a pig in a gig!
Well, I never saw a pig ride in a gig

*Child*: Where are you going, you little pig?
*4th Pig*: I'm going to the barber's to buy a wig.
*Child*: A wig, little pig!
A pig in a wig?
Why, whoever before saw a pig in a wig?

*Child*: Where are you going, you little pig?
*5th pig*: Why, I'm going to the ball to dance a fine jig.
*Child*: A jig, little pig!
A pig dance a jig!
Well, I never before saw a pig dance a jig!

*Thomas Hood*

## RUBADUBDUB!

Rubadubdub!
Rubadubdub!
Rrr-Rrr-Rubadubdub!

You'd think twenty drummers
    Were drumming to battle
        (Rubadubdub!
        Rubadubdub!)
But its really the Twins
    With two sticks and a rattle,
        Rubadub,
        Rubadubdub
        On a tub.

Rrr-Rrr-Rubadubdub!
Rrr-Rrr-Rubadubdub!
Rrr-Rrr-Rrr-Rrr-
Rrr-Rubadubdub!

*Rodney Bennett*

# HERE WE GO DANCING

Here we go dancing
Round in a ring,
Dancing and prancing
Round in a ring.

Who'll dance the longest?
Who is the strongest?
Dancing and prancing,
Round in a ring.

*Traditional*

## PADDLING

Baby and I
At the edge of the sea,
Both of us paddling,
Brave as can be.
Here comes a big wave,
Both of us run,
See, it has caught us—
Oh, isn't it fun!

*Traditional*

## THE CAMEL

Sitting on the camel.
    Round the Zoo we go,
Having jolly journeys,
    Riding to and fro.
Watching all the children,

    Sitting up so high,
Waving to the people
    As they're passing by.

Oh! The fun we're having!
    What a lovely view!
Sitting on the camel
    Going round the Zoo!

*Irene Thompson*


## A COUGH

I have a little cough, sir,
In my little chest, sir,
Every time I cough, sir,
It leaves a little pain, sir,
Cough, cough, cough, cough,
There it is again, sir.

*Robert Graves*

## ONE—TWO, BUCKLE MY SHOE!

One—two,
Buckle my shoe;

Three—four,
Shut the door;

Five—six,
Pick up sticks;

Seven—eight,
Lay them straight;

Nine—ten,
A good fat hen.

*Traditional*


## HOPPING FROG

Hopping frog, hop here and be seen,
    I'll not pelt you with stick and stone:
Your cap is laced and your coat is green;
    Goodbye, we'll let each other alone.

*Christina Rossetti*

## THE LITTLE PIGGY-WIG

A little Piggy-wig once went to court,
    To see the King and Queen:
But they said, "Little Pig, you can't come in,
    Until your face is clean."

So they wheeled him away in a wheel-barrow
    To the middle of the market place,
And they washed and washed, till there wasn't a speck
    Of dust upon his face.

Then they wheeled him back in the wheel-barrow,
    Because his face was clean;
And he took off his hat and made his bow,
    Before the King and Queen.

*D'Arcy Wentworth Thompson*

## FINGER PLAY

Ten little squirrels
    Up in a tree.
Said the first little squirrel,
    "What do we see?"
Said the second little squirrel,
    "A man with a gun!"
Said the third little squirrel,
    "Let's run! Let's run!"

Said the fourth little squirrel,
    "Let's hide in the shade."
Said the fifth little squirrel,
    "Ho, who's afraid?"
But BANG went the gun,
And how they did run!

*Anonymous*

# MR MINNITT

Mr Minnitt mends my soles
When I have walked them into holes.
He works in such a funny place
And has a wrinkly, twinkly face.
His hands are brown and hard and thin,
His thread goes slowly out and in,
He cannot walk without a crutch—
I like him very, very much.

*Rose Fyleman*

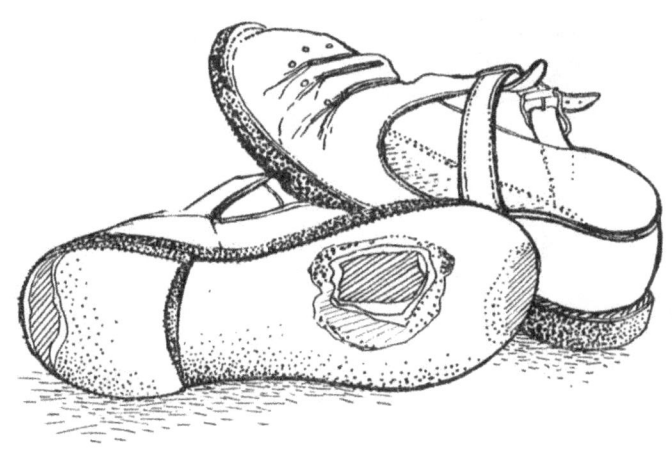

## THE GOBLIN

A goblin lives in our house,
In our house, in our house,
A goblin lives in our house
All the year round.
He bumps
And he jumps
And he thumps
And he stumps.
He knocks
And he rocks
And he rattles at the locks.
A goblin lives in our house,
In our house, in our house,
A goblin lives in our house
All the year round.

*Rose Fyleman*

## HARK! HARK! THE DOGS DO BARK!

Hark! Hark! The dogs do bark,
The beggars are coming to town;
Some in rags and some in tags,
And some in a silken gown.
Some gave them white bread,
And some gave them brown,
Some gave them a good horse-whip,
And sent them out of the town.

*Traditional*


## IS JOHN SMITH WITHIN?

"Is John Smith within?"
    "Yes, that he is."
"Can he mend a shoe?
    "Aye, marry, too,
    Here a nail, there a nail,
    Tick, tack, too."

*Traditional*

## FINGER GAME — I

Put your finger in Foxy's hole,
Foxy is not at home;
Foxy is at the back door,
Picking at a bone.

*Traditional*


## FINGER GAME — II

Dance, Thumbkin, dance,
Dance, ye merry men, every one;
For Thumbkin, he can dance alone,
Thumbkin he can dance alone.

Dance, Foreman, dance,
Dance, ye merry men, every one;
For Foreman, he can dance alone,
Foreman, he can dance alone.

Dance, Longman, dance,
Dance, ye merry men, everyone;
For Longman, he can dance alone,
Longman, he can dance alone.

Dance Ringman, dance,
Dance ye merry men, every one;
For Ringman, he can dance alone,
Ringman, he can dance alone.

Dance Littleman, dance,
Dance ye merry men, every one;
For Littleman, he can't dance alone,
Littleman, he can't dance alone.

*Traditional*

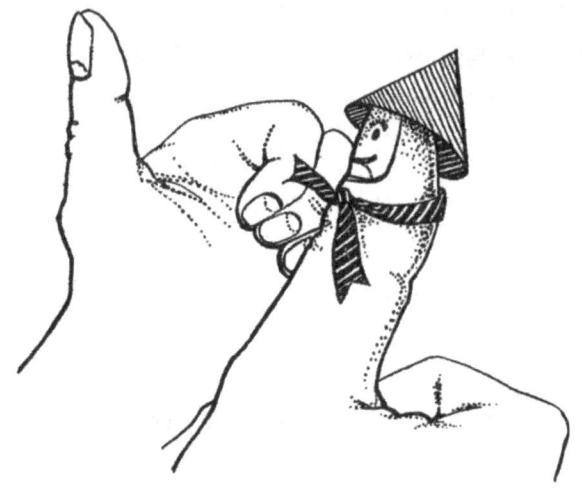

## A FACE GAME

Knock at the knocker,  *(forehead)*
Pull the bell,  *(ear)*
Peep through the keyhole,  *(eyes)*
Lift the latch  *(nose)*
And walk in!  *(mouth)*

*Traditional*


## HERE WE GO! (*A Dance*)

He we go up, up, up.
And here we go down, down, down;
And here we go backwards and forwards,
And here we go round and round.

*Traditional*


## WHEN I WAS A LADY!

When I was a lady, a lady, a lady,
When I was a lady, oh, this way went I!
Oh, this way went I! Oh, this way went I!
When I was a lady, oh, this way went I!

*Traditional*

## AT PLAY

I like to skip,
I like to jump,
I like to run about;
I like to play,
I like to sing,
I like to laugh and shout!
So we'll all
    Skip,
        Jump,
            Run,
Play and laugh and shout,
Till Mummy comes out
And Daddy comes out,
To see—to see
What it's all about!

*Winifred Kingdon-Ward*

## DANCE IN A RING

Dance in a ring,
Dance in a ring—
Round and round we go;
We will shout
And we will sing
As round and round we go;
Dance and shout,
Shout and sing
As round and round we go.

*Winfred Kingdon-Ward*

## THE DRUM

Listen! Listen!
Come-come-come!
Hark to the beat
Of the great big drum!
Come in ones
And come in twos
(And mind you wear
Your proper shoes);
Come in twos
And come in threes
Lift your feet
And bend your knees;
Hark! Hark!
Come-come-come!
Keep time to the beat
Of the great big drum!

*Winfred Kingdon Ward*

## HEIGH-HO!

There was a little rose in a garden bed,
She had a green frock and a pretty pink head.
Heigh Ho!
Let the winds blow.

There came a little bee and he said: "Fair lady,
You live in a garden sweet and shady."
Heigh Ho!
Let the winds blow.

"Fair Sir," said the rose, "you bring warm weather;
Pray let us sing a gay song together."
Heigh Ho!
Let the winds blow.

There came a little bird and he said: "I'll stay
And sing a right merry song, if I may."
Heigh Ho!
Let the winds blow.

There came a little girl, and she danced and said:
"I love my rose with the pretty pink head."
Heigh Ho!
Let the winds blow.

She danced and sang in the garden shady,
Good-bye bird and bee; good-bye rose-lady.
Heigh Ho!
Let the winds blow.

*M. Ashworth*


## SONG FOR A BALL-GAME

Bounce ball! Bounce ball!
One-two-three.
Underneath my right leg
And round about my knee
Bounce ball! Bounce ball!
Bird-or-bee
Flying from the rosebud
Up into the tree.

Bounce ball! Bounce ball!
Fast as you go
Underneath my left leg
And round about my toe,
Bounce ball! Bounce ball!
Butt-er-fly
Flying from the rosebud
Up into the sky.

Bounce ball! Bounce ball!
You can't stop.
Right leg and left leg
Round them both you hop.
Bounce ball! Bounce ball!
Shy-white-dove,
Tell me how to find him,
My own true love.

*Winfred Thorley*

## CLAPPING RHYME

Chatter, chatter,
What a clatter!
Clap your hands,
It doesn't matter!

*Mona Swann*


## LOOBY LOO

Here we go looby loo,
    Here we go looby light,
Here we go looby loo
    All on a Saturday night.

Put your right hand in—
    Put your right hand out—
Shake it a little,
    And turn yourself about.

*Traditional*

## WHEN THE WIND IS IN THE EAST

When the wind is in the East,
'Tis neither good for man nor beast;
When the wind is in the North,
The skilful fisher goes not forth,
When the wind is in the South,
It blows the bait in the fish's mouth;
When the wind is in the West,
Then 'tis at the very best.

*Traditional*


## SKIPPING

If you can skip
On the tip of your toes,
I'll give you a ribbon
To tie into bows.
Skip! skip!
For everyone knows
It's easy to skip
On the tip of your toes.

*Ruth Large*

## WALKING WITH A SWING

Follow-my-leader, follow-my-leader,
Follow-my-leader after me.
Follow me up to the top of the hill,
And follow me down to the sea.

*Clive Sansom*


## RUNNING

Run, run, run, run,
Have a little fun—
In and out the shadows
And in and out the sun
   (*Repeat*)

*Ruth Large*

## STIRRING

Stir the soup in the pot,
Make it nice and hot,
Round and round and round and round,
Stir the soup in the pot.

*Ruth Large*


## GALLOPING

Gallop, pony, gallop now,
Gallop, gallop, ho!
Gallop, pony, gallop now,
Whoa! Whoa! Whoa!

*Clive Sansom*


## MARCHING

Let, right, left, right,
Hear the tramping feet;
A regiment has come to town,
Marching down the street.

*Traditional*

## TING-A-LING-BONE!

Ting-a-ling bone! Ting-a-ling bone!
A fire broke out in the little goat's home.
A pailful of water was fetched by the hen
To put out the fire if she could, and then
The dogs from the farm-house came as well,
They were bringing a ladder and ringing a bell.
Ting-a-ling bone! Ting-a-ling bone!
We'll put out the fire in the little goat's home.

*Traditional*


## WHY IS PUSSY IN BED?

"Why is Pussy in bed?
    "She is sick," says the Fly,
    "And I fear she will die,
And that's why she's in bed."

"Who makes her nice gruel
    That she may not get worse?"
    "Dog Tray is her nurse,
And makes her nice gruel."

"Who thinks she'll get better?"
   "I do," said the Deer,
   "And I thought so last year.
I think she'll get better.

And when Puss is quite well
   She shall have the best fare,
   She shall have the best fare,
And we'll ring the great bell."

*Traditional*

# KINGS CAME RIDING

Kings came riding,
One, two and three,
Over the desert
And over the sea.

One in a ship
With a silver mast;
The fisherman wondered
As he went past.

One on a horse
With a saddle of gold;
The children came running
To behold.

One came walking,
Over the sand,
With a casket of treasure
Held in his hand.

All the people
Said "where go they?"
But the kings went forward
All through the day.

Night came on
As those kings went by;
They shone like the gleaming
Stars in the sky.

*Charles Williams*

## BOUNCE THE BALL

Bounce the ball,
Bounce the ball,
Up in the air we throw the ball.
If we do it rightly,
We hold the ball tightly.
Bounce the ball,
Bounce the ball,
Up in the air we throw the ball,
Holding the ball
Tightly.

*Freda Parsons*

## CLAPPING GAME

Pease pudding hot
Pease pudding cold
Pease pudding in the pot
Nine days old.
Some like it hot
Some like it cold
Some like it in the pot
Nine days old.

*Traditional*


## SING ME A SONG

Sing me a song—
What shall I sing?
Three merry sisters
Dancing in a ring,
Light and fleet upon their feet,
As birds upon the wing.

*Christina Rossetti*

# THE ANIMALS AND THE ARK

1. The animals went in one by one,
    Hurrah! hurrah!
The animals went in one by one,
    Hurrah! hurrah!
The animals went in one by one—
The elephant chewing a carroway bun;
    And they all went into the Ark,
    For to get out of the rain.

2. The animals went in two by two,
    Hurrah! hurrah!
The animals went in two by two,
    Hurrah! hurrah!
The animals went in two by two—
The centipede and the kangaroo;
    And they all went into the Ark,
    For to get out of the rain.

*(Repeat with..."three by three,", "four by four" etc., changing line six as shown below.)*

3. The pig, the rabbit and the chimpanzee.
4. The great hippopotamus stuck in the door.
5. "Step along smartly! Look alive!"
6. The monkeys were up to their usual tricks.
7. Said the ant to the antelope "Who are you shovin' "
8. The worm was early, the bird was late.
9. They all formed fours and marched in line.
10. If you want any more, you must start it again.

*Traditional*


## HAMMERING

Strong is our arm,
And heavy we can strike,
With a bang on the hammer
And a clang on the spike.

*Clive Sansom*

## WHO'S THAT RINGING?

Who's that ringing at the front-door bell?
    Meow! Meow! Meow!
I'm a little black kitty,
And I'm not very well.
    Meow! Meow! Meow!
Then dip your pretty nose
In this little bowl of fat.
    Meow? Meow? Meow?
But that is far the quickest way
To cure a little kitty-cat.
Meow? Meow? Meow?

*Traditional*

# TEACHING NOTES

## *BOOK ONE*

# PART ONE: POEMS TO SPEAK

## Trumpet and Drum
After giving a first reading of the poem whilst the class listens, the teacher might introduce activity. The poem can be read aloud by the class in chorus and the action of beating a drum initiated during the reading of 'rub-a-dub-dub' in lines 1 and 3 of verse two. Several students can then be brought to the front of the class and asked to identify themselves with Michael by marching to and fro and imitating the beating movement. Whilst this is done, one group can be asked to say the first 'rub-a-dub; another can be given 'boom! zoom! zoom!' and a third group the second 'rub-a-dub-dub'—the teacher narrating the rest of the poem. The imitative beating movement can be varied with actual desk-tapping and there are possibilities for varied group arrangements.

## Fishes
Different students can say the numbers in the first line; the class might speak lines 2 and 4 in chorus and the teacher or a group of students might ask the question in line 3.

## Ding, Dong, Bell
Half the class can say the first line, whilst the other half 'pull' the bell. A small group might say lines 2 and 4, whilst the teacher or a pupil asks the question in line 3.

## Hop, Hop, Hop

One or two students can be asked to hop in front of the class; one group can be asked to say, 'Little bird, will you stop, stop, stop...' Another group can ask, 'How do you do?' and the teacher can narrate the rest of the verse.

## Knock at the Door

The vocabulary is more difficult than for the first poem, but the approach can be similar. A first reading by the teacher can be followed by a chorus reading from the whole class and then, whilst the teacher narrates most of the poem, different groups or individuals can be asked to say the lines 'Come in, Mr Wind' and 'What's that, Mr Wind?' Because of the language difficulty, this poem is best chosen for a first year class in which there are students with pre-school knowledge of English. Some explanation of certain words is necessary and perhaps this could be done before the poetry lesson in a language lesson.

*Rattles*: giving out a rapid succession of short, sharp, hard sounds.
*Blind*:   a screen for a window, usually on a roller.

## The Moon

Useful for practice after a lesson on vowel sounds. This verse can also be used as material to improve expression (or intonation) and oral resonance.

## Timothy Two

The teacher can narrate this poem except for the line, 'I'll soon get you!'...which can be said by the whole class. This verse can be used for practice work after a Speech lesson which has dealt with vowel sounds, particularly 'u' (*oo*).

## Oh Where and Oh Where?
One group can ask the question in the first line, a second group the question in the second line and a third group the question in the last line. The whole class can say line 3.

## Where are you going, My Little Cat?
The '*ae*' as in 'sat' can be practised. One student can leave the room and enter it again and be asked by the class the question in the first two lines. The student should answer the question (lines 3 and 4) and three different groups can then say the last three lines.

## The Rain
Good for practice of the diphthong '*ei*'.

## A Rhyme for Washing Hands
The class should stand and, whilst the teacher reads, the students can desk-tap during line 1 and clap hands during line 3. One or two students at the front of the class can imitate pushing a plough.

## Hey, Diddle, Diddle
The teacher speaks the words to the class several times. The students can then be divided into two groups—one group to read the first three lines, the other group to read the rest of the poem.

Later, a scene can be enacted at the front of the class in which different students play the parts of the cow, the dog, and the dish, whilst the rest of the class speaks the whole poem.

## My Toys
Here is a good poem for varied group work. The teacher can read the verse except for the imitative sounds. Thus, in a mixed class, the girls might be given 'chuff-chuff-choo'

and 'rum-tum-tum,' whilst the boys could say 'grr...grr...grr' and 'clitter-clatter-clitter-clatter, rattle-bang'. The whole class could join together for the final 'BUMP!'

Many other arrangements are possible, as the teacher will easily see.

## A Riddle

After a first reading, students can be asked to suggest answers. The traditional answer is: *a star*.

## Hide and Seek

One group of students can read this poem whilst the game is played by others in the class. Students can play in turns.

## Three Little Kittens

The class can be the kittens and the teacher their mother, and there is plenty of opportunity for varied grouping. A small section of the class can mime some of the more obvious actions.

## To Let

Before this poem is read the teacher can start a short discussion about chickens, for example, "Tell me about the chickens your father has. Do you get many eggs?" The teacher can then read the poem to the class, tapping the stressed syllables with his or her finger on the table. After a first reading the class can join the teacher; reading aloud and tapping and taking the time from him or her. After some practice, the words 'tap! tap! tap!' and 'crack! crack! crack!' can be said by individuals or by a group.

This poem is useful for practice of the sound 'ae' (*a* as in 'sat'). The word 'fret' will need explaining in its context.

## How Many Days Has My Baby To Play?
A useful little verse for practicing initial consonants, particularly '*s*' and '*m*'. The teacher can ask the question in the first line and the students can answer individually or in groups.

## Pussy Cat and Pussy Dog
This little poem offers good practice in the pronunciation of consonant sounds and also the sounds 'aeu' (*ow* as in 'now') 'ə' ('er' as in 'her') 'i' ('*i*' as in 'sit') and 'ae' ('*a*' as in 'sat'). The actions of stroking and patting can be mimed, and there is opportunity for individual and group work.

## Ding-Dong! Ting-A-Ling
Pulling bell ropes can be mimed. The teacher might ask different groups the question in line 2 and each group can answer with lines 1, 3 and 4. The concentration here, of course, is on 'ŋ' (*ng* as in 'long').

## Sheep and Lambs
Primarily for practice of the vowel 'a' (as in 'far', 'calm'). One small group can be the Lambs, another group can be their Mothers.

## Drowsy Flies
Mr Rodney Bennett devised this little verse for work on sibilant consonants—'hissers' and 'buzzers' as he calls them. The word 'drowsy' will need explanation.

## A Little Tale
This could be combined with the poem *To Let* on page 21, and the same background discussion should serve. The difficult 'ʌ' ('*u*' as in 'but') sound can be introduced or revised.

## If I Met
More practice for the sounds 'a' (as in 'far') and 'ei' (*ay* as in 'rain'). The teacher can read lines, 1, 3 and 5, whilst groups can be given lines 2, 4, and 6. Pictures of the two animals and the bird would be very useful to arouse interest beforehand.

## The Three Little Pigs
This is suitable for a good class in the second year. There is an opportunity for dramatization with speech and also for mime during a reading aloud session. Whilst the actions are being mimed by a small group the teacher can narrate the story except for, 'umph! umph! umph!' and 'wee! wee! wee!' which can be given to the rest of the class. Speech can be added to the dramatization in the second verse ('My dear little brothers', etc.).

*Sty*    enclosure for pigs.
*Brat*    child (in a rather contemptuous sense).
*Moral*    the guidance which can be inferred from a fable, story or incident.

## "Bow-wow," Says the Dog
Different groups can say the sounds the birds and animals make. The sounds could be imitated and toy animals and birds or pictures of them would add to the interest. For practice of 'mju' (as in 'music'); 'æu' (*ow* as in 'now'), 'u' (*oo* as in 'moon'); 'æ' (*a* as in 'sat') ə as in 'more'); '^' (*u* as in 'but'), and 'i' (*ee* as in 'seat,' 'meet').

## Tippy Tiptoe
For practising the 'i' sound. The teacher and most of the class say the lines whilst a small group mimes the actions suggested in the poem.

## Just Like Me
Frequent repetition of the 'i'('ee' as in 'meet') sound. Five individuals in the class could say the lines, one after the other, and the rest of the class could say the refrain. Alternatively, five students in chorus could say line 1, four students line 3, three students line 5, two students line 7, and one student line 9. The chorus might begin loudly and gradually diminish in volume, or vice-versa. The last 'Just like me,' however, can be the grand climax.

## Blow the Fire
Whilst half the class says the whole poem, the rest of the students can blow quietly after each line has been spoken. This should be done rhythmically and timed so that the students blow together.

## The Crow
Consonantal practice, principally 'k'. The teacher can read most of the poem, leaving the children to imitate the bird sounds.

## Bells Go Ding-Dong!
Good practice for 'ŋ' (*ng* as in 'long'). For this sound the back of the tongue is against the back of the palate; the soft palate lowers and the sound is sent through the nose. A group can imitate bell-ringing whilst the majority of the class say the lines.

## Hammer, Hammer, Hammer
Half the class can say the poem, whilst the other half mimes the action of hammering. Later the whole class can say the lines and mime the actions simultaneously.

## The Ferryman
Practice in the vowel-sound 'u' (*oo* as in 'moon'). The lines spoken by the Maid and the Ferryman can be said alternatively by class and teacher, by two students or by two groups.

## The Song of the Engine
Suitable for a class in the second year. Half the class can read the first two verses, whilst the other half takes verses 3 and 4. Verses 1 and 2 should be said slowly, and in particular, there should be distinct pauses as indicated by the dashes in verse 2. The lines in verses 3 and 4 should be taken more quickly with the climax in verse 4. The words 'laboured' and 'track' might need preliminary explanation.

## Windy Nights
This poem is suitable for a good class in the second year. The class can say the last line in each verse in chorus as the teacher reads the poem for a second time. Later the class can be divided into two groups. Group One might say the first two lines in each verse, whilst Group Two speaks the second two lines in both verses. Line 5, in each case, could be spoken by the teacher and line 6 by the whole class.

After a further reading by the teacher, a discussion can follow with some simple questions, for example:

1. Does the man ride in the daytime or at night?
2. When are the fires out?
3. Does the man's horse walk, trot or gallop?
4. Which is quicker – walking, trotting, or galloping?
5. When are ships tossed at sea?

## The Squirrel
To practice 'ə' (*'ir'* as in 'bird'; *'er'* as in 'her'); 'I' ('i' as in 'sit'); 'ei' (*ay* as in 'say', 'rain') and 'æu' (*ow* as in 'now') If there is sufficient space, half the students in the

class can hop in time to the reading of the other half. The '*h*' of 'hippity' should be sounded clearly to give good breath control practice. The last verse can be taken quite speedily with a great shout on the last line, 'OUT IT FELL!'

## Wee Willie Winkie

Useful for practice of the consonants '*p* ' *d*', '*t*' and '*k*' and the diphthong 'æu' (*ow* as in 'now', 'gown').

After a first reading by the teacher, the children can be divided into three groups. One group tells the story, a second group speaks the part of Willie Winkie and students in the third group join hands in pairs to form imaginary doorways in a street. Each student from the Willie Winkie group should run lightly to a 'door' to ask the question:

'Are all the children in their beds?
It's past eight o'clock.'

## There Was an Old Woman

The teacher can narrate the story whilst the students speak the dialogue.

## Ring the Gong

Practise of 'ŋ' (*ng* as in 'long') and general help for the improvement of nasal resonance. The tip of the tongue is pressed to the lower teeth. Students can mime the ringing.

## The Old Woman in the Basket

The sounds 'u' (*oo* as in 'moon') and 'i' ('*I*' as in 'sit') can be practised. The teacher can narrate the first verse and, in a mixed class, the thrice-repeated 'Old Woman', can be said by a group of boys; the second line of the second verse can be said by the whole class and the last two lines of the second verse can be taken by a group of girls.

## Bat, Bat
To practice the labial explosive, '*b*'. This short verse can be read by the whole class after the teacher's introduction. The final '*t*' and '*n*' sounds will need careful attention.

## Plippetty, Clippetty
Very good for the '*kl*' (*cl*) and '*pl*' sounds. The whole class can read this quickly after the teacher's first reading and then the teacher can select students for individual practice.

## A Hippity Hippity Hop!
Consonants '*h*' and '*p*'. Most of the class can read the poem whilst the remaining students hop to its beat.

## Round the Roundabout
For agility work with the consonant '*r*'. Students can join hands in a circle and run lightly round to the time of the poem which can be read by the teacher and a small group.

## Tigers
For consonants '*f*', '*t*', '*p*' and '*b*'. Four groups could read a verse each.

## What Do I See?
Primarily for class practice of the '*m*' sound. The lips should be together with the teeth slightly apart and the tip of the tongue touching the lower ones. Students can be asked to feel the tickling of the lips as the sound comes out. A small group can say most of this poem except for 'hum, hum, hum' which can be taken by the whole class. 'Sing-song' should be avoided if possible. There is no need to pause or stop, for example, at the end of each line, 'A bumble-bee', where there is no stop.

## Hickety Pickety
For the '*p*' sound. Sing-song should be avoided. The whole class can speak this verse and the students can hold up nine fingers and then ten fingers for the line:
    'Sometimes nine, and sometimes ten.'

## Three Little Mice
Further practice of the unvoiced labial explosive, '*p*'. This is a useful little poem for activity work. The story can be mimed by a group of four students—three can play the parts of the mice and the fourth can be the Pussy. During the mime, the teacher can narrate the first two lines, a small group can say the Pussy's lines (3, 5, and 7) and the rest of the class can be the mice, who speak lines 4, 6 and 8. Later the poem can be dramatised with dialogue spoken by the actors.

## Another Riddle
After a reading by the teacher and then by the class the students can be asked to suggest answers. The traditional answer is: *a walnut.*

## The Goldfish
A longer poem suitable for an advanced second year class. A good poem to choose for practice of the vowel sound '*u*' (*oo* as in 'too,' 'moon'). This is a useful vowel for lip-rounding exercises. The *oo* sounds in the poem are rather long. The teacher should give a first reading and should, by emphasis, draw attention to the correct pronunciation of 'play' and 'stay' (the *ei* sound as in 'say', 'rain,' etc). It would probably be wise to confine the students' reading aloud to good, individual readers who have been given an opportunity to prepare the poem.

## As I Looked Out
Another poem for a second year class. After listening to the teacher's reading, a small group could narrate the whole poem whilst individual students take turns to mime the actions of the pig. The narrators can do the waving referred to in line five.

## Ducks
The teacher could read the first verse and four different groups of students could take each line of the second verse. The third verse could again be read by the teacher and the last line of the poem by the whole class.

## Whistle
A small group could speak most of this poem, except for line 4 of both verses which could be said by the whole class, and line 3 of the second verse which could be spoken by an individual student. After a reading in this manner and before a repetition, the students could practice whistling.

## What Does the Bee Do?
The teacher can ask the questions and the whole class, at first, can provide the answers. Later, individual students might speak the answers in turn.

## The Spider's Web
Half of the class can ask the question contained in the first two lines of each verse, while the other half gives the answers. A simple narrative poem for the second or third year.

## Clocks and Watches
Useful practice for the consonant sound 't' is provided in this little poem. The teacher can narrate, whilst the class imitates the sounds of the various timepieces. 'Tick-a-tacker, tick-a-tacker, tick-a-tacker, tick,' should, if possible,

be taken at the same speed as the 'TICK-TOCK, TICK-TOCK', of the first verse.

*Mantel clock*: the type of clock usually to be found on a shelf above a fireplace.

## Flying Kites
In a mixed class, one girl could read the first verse and one boy the second, whilst the whole class speaks the third verse. The teacher could bring a kite into the classroom to show the students at the beginning of the lessons and during the reading, two students could pretend to fly it at the front of the class.

E.B.M. Watson's verse provides useful practice of the sound 'ai' as in 'my,' 'fight', etc.

## Who Has Seen the Wind?
This poem provides useful practice for the long round sound 'u', (*oo* as in 'moon'). After a preliminary reading by the teacher, a small group could be asked to speak the question in the first line. One individual student could say the rest of the verse, the group could take the first line of the second verse and one student the remainder of it. After reading practice, drawing and painting can begin.

### PART TWO: POEMS TO ACT AND DANCE

## The Elves Dance
Whilst a small group of students speaks the poem after the teacher's preparatory reading and instructions have been given, the rest of the class can join hands in a large circle. As the poem is being read the students can skip round to the beat of the lines. Skipping can be in a clockwise direction for lines 1 and 2, then anti-clockwise for the third

and fourth lines. Students can skip to the centre on line 5, out again on line 6, in *and* out on line 7, which should be taken slowly and with the emphasis put by the readers on the important words thus:
  'All about, IN and OUT'

Clockwise skipping can be resumed during the reading of the last line.

## Incey Wincey Spider
Whilst speaking the poem, the students can perform the arm, hand and finger actions usually associated with this well-known traditional rhyme.

## The Little Mice
Useful for practice of 'p' and 's' sounds. Each student in the class can be encouraged to dramatise both these verses according to his or her own interpretation, whilst the lines are being read by a selected group. The 'playing' referred to in the first verse could be skipping or hopping or 'leap-frog', etc. Each student should like perfectly still and quiet as if asleep during the reading of the second verse. If possible, accompanying 'playing' and 'sleeping' music on a piano or other musical instrument would be useful.

## Stepping Stones
The consonant '*s*' can be practised. The tip of the tongue needs to be kept behind the lower teeth. The whole class should enjoy saying this poem, whilst a small group mime (1) crossing the river by the stones, (2) looking for the fish, and (3) wobbling on the stones before falling into the river on the final resounding 'SPLASH' (Verse 4).

## The Swing
Students can watch the swing go 'up into the air' as they speak the poem. Half the class could take the first two lines and the other half the last two.

## The Postman
For practice of '*r*' and '*t*' (used initially and finally). One group can be given the first line, a second group the second line and the fourth line; the teacher can take lines 3, 5 and 6; a third group can say line 7, and a fourth group line 8. Different individual students can mime the part of the postman in turn and the classroom door could be 'the garden gate'.

## Dickyducks
Another of Mr Rodney Bennett's excellent jingles, useful to practice and improve the pronunciation of the consonant '*k*'. A group can march to and fro whilst the majority of the class speaks the verse together.

## The Pancake
The teacher and the whole class can say the poem together while miming the actions, or, alternatively, a small group of students could be brought to the front of the class to mime, as individual students speak the lines.

## Rubadubdub!
Excellent for practice of '*r*'. The class can say this together whilst a small group marches up and down to the rhythm of the verse.

## Getting Up
A useful poem for practice of '*r*' and '*s*' sounds. The author, Miss McCrea, suggests that students can dramatise all the actions as they say the story. For the last line they can raise

both arms and lower them quickly, making running movements with their fingers.

## The Balloon Man
Mr Herbert wrote this little poem especially for active work with 'the littlest ones'. The dramatization possible is obvious from his clever arrangement of the verses.

## The Little Piggies
Excellent for practice work on consonants, particularly *'p'* and initial and final *'g'*. The first Pig could stretch up on tiptoe as he says the first line; the 2nd Pig could imitate a digging movement; the 3rd Pig could skip; the 4th Pig could walk rapidly, touching his head with his hands and the 5th Pig could execute a simple dancing movement. One individual student could play the part of the child, or the whole class could say the lines.

## Here We Go Dancing
If there is sufficient space, all the students could skip to the rhythm of this poem, whilst the teacher reads it. If the students are restricted to the classroom, two students at a time can skip in front of the desks, whilst the whole class speaks the lines.

## One—Two, Buckle My Shoe!
One pair of students can say, 'One—two, Buckle my shoe' together; a second pair, 'Three—four, shut the door', and so on down to 'my plate's empty'. Whilst the lines are being spoken, six students can be brought to the front of the class to mime the actions implied in the following lines: 'Buckle my shoe'; 'shut the door'; 'Pick up sticks'; 'lay them straight'; 'Dig and delve'; 'my plate's empty'. The following word might need explanation in the context of a sentence. (*delve*: to dig).

## Hopping Frog
'Pelt' and 'Laced' will need preliminary explanation.

> *pelt*: to fling stones, etc (at).
> *laced*: decorated with the material, lace.

A small group can imitate hopping frogs, as the rest of the class say the verse.

## Paddling
Suitable for first year classes. Students could stand at their desks and mime the actions, whilst the teacher reads the poem aloud. There need not be any 'running': students could simply take a pace back as 'the wave comes'.

## The Camel
The teacher might show the class a picture of a camel and then, whilst he speaks the poem, four students could play the part of the camel and carry a fifth child to and fro in front of the rest of the class.

## A Cough
For practice of consonant '*k*'. Two students can mime the parts of doctor and patient, while the rest of the class speaks the poem together.

## The Little Piggy-Wig
A very suitable little poem for dramatization.
*Characters*: Little Piggy-Wig; Queen; Two Attendants.
The teacher or a specially selected group could narrate the poem, except for the lines, 'Little Pig, you can't come in, Until your face is clean', which could either be said by the King and Queen together, or by two other students. The actions of the story can be mimed by the cast whilst the lines are being spoken.

### Finger Play
All the class can take part in this action poem. The lines of the poem are spoken by the students together, except for the lines 4, 6, 8, 10, and 12, which can be said by individuals or small, selected groups. Students can raise their fingers according to the numbers mentioned, e.g. ten, first, second, third, fourth, fifth. The 'BANG', of course, in the last line is a grand climax.

### Mr Minnitt
After a preliminary reading of the complete poem by the teacher, eight groups of students can take a line each. One student could mime the part of the shoemaker at the front of the class and some simple properties (such as a hammer, nails, a last and some shoes) would add interest. 'Mr Minnitt' could get up and limp away after line 7 has been read.

### The Goblin
While most of the class read lines 1 to 4, and lines 12 to 15, individual students can be given the short lines from 'he bumps' down to and including 'and he rattles at the locks.' Seven students can be chosen to mime individually the actions suggested in these lines.

### Hark! Hark! The Dogs Do Bark
Useful for practicing '$a{:}$' (as in 'far, 'master'). One group might speak aloud lines 1 and 2, another group lines 3 and 5, and a third group lines 4 and 6. The whole class could say lines 7 and 8. Other variations are possible. A number of students could be dogs and bystanders watching a procession of beggars (another group).

## Is John Smith Within?
As one student mimes the part of John Smith, the shoemaker, the teacher should read lines 1 and 3 and be answered by the rest of the class with lines 2 and 4. A separate group could speak lines 5 and 6. This poem could be read in conjunction with *Mr Minnitt*. The archaic word, 'marry' should be explained by substituting a synoym.

## Finger Game 1
Suitable for the whole class to speak aloud whilst performing the obvious finger actions.

## Finger Game 2
As for the previous poem.

## A Face Game
For class reading aloud with actions.

## Here We Go!
For all the class to say while performing the simple little dance, preferably to suitable music from a musical instrument. On the first line students can rise on to their toes; down on the second line, skipping forwards and backwards on the third, and turning round on the fourth. The dance can be done individually, or by a circle formed with joined hands.

## When I Was A Lady
The students can join hands to form a circle. The teacher could read the poem aloud whilst on the first 'oh, this way went I!' the students skip two paces to the centre; two paces back when the phrase is repeated; two paces to the left on the second repetition, and two paces to the right on the third.

## At Play

For practice of ʃ (*sh* as in 'short') and *æu* (as in 'now'). If there is suitable space, the actions can be performed by individual students in their own time as the teacher and part of the class read the poem aloud, making a pause between each of the lines to give time for the actions.

## Dance In A Ring

The students can form one or two circles and join hands. They can then speak lines 1 and 2 and skip around in a clockwise direction, whilst saying line 3. Lines 4 and 5 can be said from a standstill position and line 6 can be spoken as the students now skip round in an anti-clockwise direction. The students can skip to the centre on line 7; out again on line 8, and round once more in a clockwise direction whilst speaking line 9.

## The Drum

For practice of 'ʌ '(u as in 'shut') sound. Here is a most useful little poem with action. A group of students, or the teacher, can read whilst the rest of the class marches to the accompaniment of an actual drum played by one of the students. The actions can be performed as suggested in the context of the poem.

## Heigh Ho!

A longer poem, probably best suited to the second year. There can be some spoken dramatization. The characters are the Rose, the Bee, the Bird and the Little Girl. The teacher can narrate the poem while the dramatization takes place, except for the refrain 'Height Ho! Let the winds blow', which can be taken by the rest of the class. The conversation of the Bee, the Rose, the Bird and the Little Girl can be spoken by the characters themselves. This suggested arrangement will require careful planning and the work might be spread over two or three lessons, depending upon the abilities of the students.

## Song For A Ball Game
Here is one of the few occasions when it would be useful to ask the students to learn the poem so that it could be read without the text. If tennis balls could be provided, the students could practice the movements suggested. These movements are, of course, repeated during the second part of each verse.

## Clapping Rhyme
For practice of the 'æ' (*a* as in 'sat') sound. Can be spoken aloud by the whole of a first year class as the clapping is performed.

## Looby Loo
The first verse provides useful practice of the 'l' sound. In the second verse, which can be read aloud by everyone, there are obvious actions to be performed.

## When The Wind Is In The East
This poem could be spoken aloud by four different groups. Group One could stand in one corner of the room and say the first two lines. Group Two could stand in another corner and speak the next two lines and so on for Groups Three and Four. A reading of this poem might, perhaps, follow a geography lesson on the points of the compass. 'Bait' might need preliminary explanation.

## Skipping
If there is room the whole class can skip. Whilst the teacher speaks the verse

## Walking With A Swing
One group can say the words, whilst another group walks jauntily after a leader.

## Running
As for the previous one.

## Stirring
A small group of, say, four students might come to the front of the class to stir, whilst the rest of the students say the lines. A pot and a spoon for each of the four would add interest.

## Galloping
The movement here is only possible in a large, unrestricted space, but the children could imitate the action of pulling reins whilst speaking the verse.

## Marching
Half the class could say the lines whilst the other half march up and down.

## Ting-A-Ling-Bone
Good nasal resonance practice.
Whilst a small group narrates the lines other than the 'Ting-a-ling bone! Ting-a-ling Bone!' which can be said by the whole class, the little scene can be dramatized. The characters are the Little Goat, the Hen and the Dogs (say, four). The teacher's desk can act as a 'house'. Whilst the second line is being spoken, the Little Goat can run out of the 'house' looking for aid. The Hen can enter at the third line carrying a bucket. The Dogs then come in carrying a small ladder (if available) and a bell. The scene ends with everyone trying to put out the fire. The bucket can be

passed from hand to hand, the bell rung and imaginary water poured on the 'flames'.

## Why Is Pussy In Bed?
One group can be given the questions to ask, i.e. line 1 of verse one; lines 1 and 2 of verse two, and line 1 of verse three. The part of the Fly can be taken by an individual student who can speak lines 2, 3 and 4 of verse one and lines 3 and 4 of verse two. Another student can play Dr. Deer and can say lines 2, 3 and 4 of verse three. Dr Deer could say the first line of the last verse; a small selected group could take the first, 'She shall have the best fare', and the whole class could speak lines 3 and 4. After the spoken work had been practiced for some time the scene can be mimed by another group.

## Kings Came Riding
This poem is suitable for elementary choral work. The teacher could read the first verse to set the scene. Three separate groups might follow with verses two, three and four and the teacher might then complete the reading of the poem by speaking verses five and six, except for the 'Where go they?' in verse five, which could be said by the whole class.

The poem refers to the three princes who came from the East to visit the baby Jesus. The teacher could tell the story to the students after the poem has been read. A reading of this poem could also accompany a lesson in which the story of Jesus is being told.
*Casket*: A small box in which valuables are usually carried.

## Bounce the Ball
A small group of students could be brought to the front to mime the actions, whilst another group speaks lines 3, 4, 5, 8, 9, and 10, The rest of the class can repeat the 'Bounce the Ball' lines.

## Clapping Game
The students can clap whilst saying the lines.

## Sing Me A Song
For a change, here is a poem that the teacher might read, whilst the students listen.

## The Animals and the Ark
The poem can be narrated by the teacher and a small group of students. The other students can line up to take the various parts. Two desks may be arranged to make the entrance to the ark. Students should try to mime the appearance and movements of the various characters.

## Hammering
All the class can say this verse and mime the action at the same time.

## Who's That Ringing?
One student can be asked to say the first line whilst sitting on a chair in front of the class. The whole class repeats the 'Meow, meow, meow' lines when they occur. A second student speaks lines 3 and 4 and enters the room as the sick cat, looking sorry for himself/herself. The first student then rises from the chair and gives a plate to the 'cat' while saying lines 6, 7, 9 and 10.

    This poem provided very good practice in the formation of the sound 'mj' (as in 'mew').

## ABOUT THE EDITOR

Verner Bickley is an educationist who has led international education projects in Singapore, Burma, Indonesia, Japan, Saudi Arabia and Hong Kong. For two years, he was Chairman of Directors of the East-West Centre in Hawaii and, for ten years, was Director of the Centre's Culture Learning Institute. He has served as an adjudicator in speech and drama festivals in several countries and as President of the English-Speaking Union in Hawaii and Chairman of the English-Speaking Union in Hong Kong. He has lived and worked in Hong Kong since 1983.

Specialising in institutional linguistics, language pedagogy and international education, Dr Bickley has written extensively on language and culture and on language learning and teaching. He has served as announcer and actor in radio and TV programmes broadcast in several Asian and Pacific countries. His voice was heard regularly over the NHK in Tokyo, the Burma Broadcasting Service, Radio Republic Indonesia and Radio Malaya where he broadcast from Singapore as newsreader and as actor and narrator in radio drama, as well as in programmes for schools and colleges.

Among the dozens of scripts he has written were five in a series on the use of poetry in the language class, broadcast in BBC radio's "Listen and Teach" series. Twenty scripts written by Dr Bickley for the Japan Broadcasting Company were broadcast as the television series, "How English Works".

His books include *Reading and Interpretation* (co-authored), *Reading and Understanding* (co-authored), *A New Malayan Songbook* (co-authored), *Easy English*, *Cultural Relations in the Global Community*, *Searching for Frederick* (an autobiographical-biographical narrative), *Language and the Young Learner in Hong Kong*, and *Forward to Beijing*. The first volume of his autobiography entitled, *Footfalls Echo in the Memory*, was published in 2010.

Born in Cheshire, England, Dr Bickley received two bachelor's degrees from the University of Wales, befor earning an M.A. degree in education there. He was made a Licentiate of the Royal Aademy of Music (Speech and Drama) in 1955 and a Licentiate of the Guildhall School of Music and Drama in the same year. He was awarded a PhD in socio-linguistics by the University of London in 1966. He is a Fellow of the Royal Society of Arts.

Employed by the British Council for twelve years, he moved from university teaching and advisory assignments to the position of English Language Officer for Japan and First Secretary in the Cultural Department of the British Embassy in Tokyo.

Dr Bickley was founding Director of the Hong Kong Government's Institute of Language in Education (which was incorporated into the Hong Kong Institute of Education after his retirement) and an Assistant Director of Education.

Dr Bickley was made a Member of the Order of the British Empire in 1964.

## ABOUT PROVERSE HONG KONG

Proverse Hong Kong, co-founded by Gillian and Verner Bickley, is based in Hong Kong, with strong regional and international connections.

Verner Bickley has headed cultural and educational centres, departments, institutions and projects in many parts of the world. Gillian Bickley has recently concluded a career as a university teacher of English Literature, spanning four continents. Proverse Hong Kong draws on their combined academic, administrative and teaching experience as well as varied long-term participation in reading, research, writing, editing, reviewing, publishing and authorship.

Proverse Hong Kong has published novels, novellas, non-fiction (including fictionalised autobiography, history, memoirs, sport, travel narratives), single-author poetry collections, and academic and young teen books. Other interests include biography, diaries, and academic works in the humanities, social sciences, cultural studies, linguistics and education. Some Proverse books have accompanying audio texts. Proverse editors work with texts by non-native-speaker writers of English as well as by native English-speaking writers.

Proverse welcomes authors who have a story to tell, wisdom, perceptions or information to convey, a person they want to memorialise, a neglect they want to remedy, a record they want to correct, a strong interest which they want to share, skills they want to teach, and who consciously seek to make a contribution to society in an informative, interesting and well-written way.

The name, *Proverse*, combines the words "prose" and "verse" and is pronounced accordingly.

## THE INTERNATIONAL PROVERSE PRIZE FOR UNPUBLISHED BOOK-LENGTH FICTION, NON-FICTION OR POETRY

The Proverse Prize, an annual international competition for an unpublished single-author book-length work of fiction, non-fiction, or poetry, the original work of the entrant, submitted in English (unpublished translations welcomed) was established in January 2008. It is open to all who are at least eighteen on the date they sign the entry form and without restriction of nationality, residence or citizenship.

Founded by Gillian and Verner Bickley, the objectives of the prize are: to encourage excellence and / or excellence and usefulness in publishable written work in the English Language, which can, in varying degrees, "delight and instruct". Entries are invited from anywhere in the world.

### The Prize
1) Publication by Proverse Hong Kong, with
2) Cash prize of HKD10,000 (HKD7.80 = approx. USD1.00)

**Proverse Prize Winners whose work has already been published by Proverse Hong Kong**
2009: Laura Solomon, Rebecca Jane Tomasis
2010: Gillian Jones
2011: David Diskin, Peter Gregoire
2012: Sophronia Liu, Birgit Bunzel Linder
2013: James McCarthy
2014: Celia Claase, Philip Chatting
2015: (Scheduled) Lawrence Gray, Gustav Preller

**Extent of the Manuscript**: within the range of what is usual for the genre of the work submitted. However, it is advisable that novellas be in the range, 30,000 to 45,000 words; other fiction (e.g. novels, short-story collections) and non-fiction (e.g. autobiographies, biographies, diaries, letters, memoirs, essay collections, etc.) should be in the range, 75,000 to 100,000 words. Poetry collections should be in the range, 5,000 to 25,000 words. Other word-counts and mixed-genre submissions are not ruled out.

**International Proverse Prize Annual Entry Deadlines**
(subject to confirmation and/or change)

| | |
|---|---|
| Receipt of Entry Fees / Entry Forms begins | [Variable, no later than] 14 April |
| Deadline for receipt of Entry Fees / Entry Forms | 31 May |
| Receipt of entered manuscripts begins | 1 May |
| Deadline for receipt of entered manuscripts | 30 June |

**The above information is for guidance only. More information, updated from time to time, is available on the Proverse website: proversepublishing.com**

## THE INTERNATIONAL PROVERSE POETRY PRIZE
## (SINGLE POEMS)

An annual international Proverse Poetry Prize (for single poems) was established in 2016. The international Proverse Poetry Prize is open to all who are at least eighteen years old whatever their residence, nationality or citizenship.

Single poems, submitted in English, are invited on (a) <u>any subject or theme, chosen by the writer</u> OR (b) <u>on a subject or theme selected by the organizers</u>.

Poems may be in any form, style or genre. Each poem should be no more than 30 lines.

Entries should previously be unpublished in any way (except in the case of unpublished translations into English of the entrant's own work already published in another language, providing the entrant holds the copyright).

**In 2016
cash prizes were offered as follows:
1st prize; USD100.00; 2nd prize: USD45.00;
3rd prizes (up to four winners): USD20.00.**

If there are enough good entries in any year, an anthology of prize-winners and selected other entries will be published.

In 2016, judging took place at the same time as the judging for the Proverse Prize for unpublished book-length fiction, non-fiction or poetry.

Judges: anonymous (as for the Proverse Prize for an unpublished book-length work).

Number of entries per person: No maximum.

No poet may win more than one prize.

Entry period: 7 May - 14 July annually.

**The above information is for guidance only.
More information, updated from time to time, is available on the Proverse website:
proversepublishing.com**

Poems to Enjoy: Book 1 (Third Edition)

## EDUCATIONAL BOOKS FROM PROVERSE

**Jockey**, by Gillian Bickley (when Gillian Workman). Hong Kong, 1979. Pbk. 64pp.
ISBN-10: 962-85570-3-3; ISBN-13: 978-962-85570-3-5.

**Poems to Enjoy: Book 1**, Edited by Verner Bickley. HK & UK: 2012. Pbk. 136 pp. (inc. 35 b/w original line-drawings & Teacher's and Student's Notes). With audio CDs. ISBN 978-988-8167-54-8.

**Poems to Enjoy: Book 2**, Edited by Verner Bickley. HK & UK: 2013. Pbk. 136pp. (inc. 37 b/w original line-drawings & Teacher's and Student's Notes). With audio CDs. ISBN 978-988-8167-51-7.

**Poems to Enjoy: Book 3**, Edited by Verner Bickley. HK & UK: 2013. Pbk. 166 pp. (inc. 39 b/w original line-drawings & Teacher's and Student's Notes). w. audio CDs. ISBN 978-988-19934-1-0.

**Poems to Enjoy: Book 4**, Edited by Verner Bickley. HK & UK: scheduled, 2014. Pbk. *c.*174 pp. (inc. *c.*41 b/w original line-drawings & Teacher's and Student's Notes).
With audio CDs. ISBN 978-988-8167-50-0.

**Poems to Enjoy: Book 5**, Edited by Verner Bickley. HK & UK: scheduled, 2015. Pbk. *c.*200 pp. (inc. *c.*36 b/w original line-drawings & Teacher's and Student's Notes).
With audio CD(s) / DVD(s). ISBN 978-988-8167-49-4.

**Spanking Goals and Toe Pokes: Football Sayings Explained**, by T. J. Martin. HK & UK, 2008. ISBN-13: 978-988-99668-2-9.

**Teachers' and Students' Guide to the Book and Audio Book, 'The Golden Needle: the Biography of Frederick Stewart (1836-1889)'.** Proverse Hong Kong Study Guides. E-book. ISBN-10: 962-85570-9-2; ISBN-13: 978-962-35570-9-7. 24Reader e-book edition (2010), ISBN-13: 978-988-19320-5-1.

**FIND OUT MORE ABOUT OUR AUTHORS AND BOOKS**

**Visit our website**
<www.proversepublishing.com>
**Visit our distributor's website**
<www.chineseupress.com>

**Follow us on Twitter**
Follow news and conversation:
<twitter.com/Proversebooks>
**OR**
Copy and paste the following to your browser window and follow the instructions:
https://twitter.com/#!/ProverseBooks
**"Like" us on www.facebook.com/ProversePress**

**Request our E-Newsletter**
Send your request to info@proversepublishing.com.

**Availability**
Most titles are available in Hong Kong and world-wide from our Hong Kong based Distributor,
The Chinese University Press of Hong Kong,
The Chinese University of Hong Kong, Shatin, NT,
Hong Kong SAR, China. Web: chineseupress.com
All titles are available from Proverse Hong Kong
and the Proverse Hong Kong UK-based Distributor.

We have stock-holding retailers in Hong Kong, Singapore (Select Books), Canada (Elizabeth Campbell Books), Principality of Andorra (Llibreria La Puça, La Llibreria). Orders can be made from bookshops in the UK and elsewhere.

**Ebooks**
Most of our titles are available also as Ebooks.

www.ingramcontent.com/pod-product-compliance
Lightning Source LLC
Chambersburg PA
CBHW070334180426
43196CB00050B/2636